YOUTHFUL
AGING SECRETS

How to
Live
Better
for
Longer

MARY JAKSCH

ISBN: 9780473447274

TABLE OF CONTENTS

The New Paradigm Of Youthful Aging

*A*re you afraid of aging? You are not alone. Most people in their 50s and 60s begin to dread getting older. They are scared of getting sick, becoming weaker, or even losing their minds.

What if you could stop or even reverse the process of aging?

Imagine what it would be like to get your body back, to sharpen your mind, and to get those creative juices flowing again? What would it feel like to know you are a valuable member of society?

Recent scientific research in rejuvenation biotechnology shows we can reset the clock and slow or even reverse aging. Scientists are developing strategies for undoing the damage caused by aging to restore youthful function to the human body and mind. It's not only medical interventions that can slow or halt the process of aging. Specific lifestyle changes can also reverse aspects of aging—even on a cellular level.

In this book, you will find inspiring stories of people who have accomplished remarkable things in their mature years.

It's no wonder most people fear old age. After all, we've been universally conditioned to think that mature age is a time of decline and disrespect.

I remember going to a restaurant with my British mother who was then in her late 80s.

The waitress looked at me and said, "What would your mum like to order?"

My mother drew herself up to her full height and exclaimed in her upper-class accent honed at Cambridge University, "Are you asking my daughter what I would like to order?"

A hush fell in the restaurant.

The waitress blushed and then gave my mother the attention and respect she deserved.

Does this sound familiar?

My mother's story is just one of many examples of disrespect for mature people. The underlying cause is the accepted view that aging makes a person less valuable.

Western society sees aging as a downward spiral where physical power, mental ability, and overall health decline. A mature person is often seen as a lesser human being, and this view is mirrored in the way older people are treated.

However, this view is changing.

There is a new paradigm of aging that sees the later part of life as a chapter of vitality, creativity, happiness, and fulfillment. I call this new paradigm *youthful aging*. This novel blueprint for aging youthfully is based on our positive plasticity, the innate capacity of human beings to adapt, change, and grow at any age.

The idea to write this book came to me on my birthday.

I was training in a karate class for Black Belts. At the end of the class, I turned to my neighbor. "Al," I said, "the next Black Belt class is going to be challenging."

"Why?" he said.

"It's my birthday next week and, as you know, the tradition is that you have to do your age in pushups."

"How old are you going to be?" Al said.

"70."

Al's jaw dropped. "What? You must be joking; you can't be 70 years old!"

"I am. My birthday's next week and I'll have to do 70 pushups," I said.

He thought for a moment. Then he said, "Well, I suppose you could do them on your knees."

"On my knees?" I shot back. "Certainly not! I wouldn't be seen dead doing pushups on my knees!"

Over the following days, I practiced pushups every morning. I was determined to do perfect, military-style pushups all the way through. And then the moment came. After the grueling two-hour Black Belt class, my teacher, Hanshi Andy Barber, called me to the front of the class. He pointed to the floor and said, "Let's see your birthday pushups!"

Everyone in the class started counting out loud. As I passed 50, and then 60, the count got louder and louder. Finally, I ground out the last few pushups and completed my 70th one. The whole dojo erupted with cheers and clapping.

Later, fellow students came to congratulate me. Some of the super-fit guys in their 20s said, "I couldn't complete 70 pushups. And I definitely can't imagine doing pushups like that when I'm your age."

"Why not?" I said. "All you have to do is keep going—and then rev up!"

It was a shock to find that these young men had already narrowed their expectations of the later stages of life. After all, studies have shown that our body fulfills our negative—as well as our positive— expectations. If someone expects to be weak and decrepit at 70, this is what is going to happen.

But equally, if someone expects to be doing karate—and 70 pushups—at 70, this is most likely where they're heading!

And with the help of 13 inspiring case studies, I'm going to show you how.

The life stories of the *youthful agers* in these case studies will inspire you. Each one reveals their secrets for enjoying a vital, energetic, connected, and fulfilling life at any age.

Youthful agers are people past retirement age who have the mental or physical capability of others who are decades younger.

I am a *youthful ager*. At 70, I feel more vitally alive than I did ten years ago. I am fitter, more productive, more creative, and more joyful than at any previous time in my life. I hope that my series of books on *youthful aging* will inspire you and guide you to experience the same zest for life that makes me jump out of bed in the mornings.

I promise this book will change the trajectory of your life. You will end up with a completely new vision of what your mature years can be like. The new paradigm of *youthful aging* will help you to bloom into full glory, at any stage of your life.

"The longer I live, the more beautiful life becomes"
~ Frank Lloyd Wright

In the next chapter, you'll find out about Charles Eugster, who said about life at 90, "It's absolutely marvelous, it's stupendous, it's terrific, amazing, exciting, glorious!" Read on to find out how he turned his life around and became a *youthful ager.*

YOUTHFUL AGING SECRETS

2 *Are Your Best Years Ahead?*

When Charles was widowed at age 82, his life started to unravel. Struggling with grief after the sudden death of his wife, Elsie, he was at a low ebb. He shuffled around in slippers or just sat in his armchair, staring out of the window at the fading light.

In his book *Age is Just a Number*, Charles Eugster recounts the following:

"As a widower, whenever I looked into the future I could not see beyond a handful of bleak and final years. Alone in the house, and conscious that my body was seriously failing me, I became convinced that I would die at 85. I had little to live for, it seemed, and duly began to wind down."

Charles sank into a depression after the loss of his wife. Hopelessness enveloped him like a dark cloud suffocating all vitality. Until then, Charles had still been publishing a newsletter for dentists, but, after

Elsie's fatal car accident, he no longer had the heart to continue. What had been a burning passion now seemed like a chore. His life was dominated by what was no longer there.

Clinging to a semblance of normal life after his loss, Charles Eugster continued to attend some training sessions at his rowing club. However, his muscles were wasting away, and he was putting on weight. The lack of work and diminishing physical abilities combined to cast him adrift with no purpose and no goals.

Then, one day, everything changed.

As he was passing a mirror, Charles caught sight of himself. Shocked by the reflection of the stooped, demoralized old man staring back at him, he decided to pick himself up and take steps to reinvigorate his life.

His first step was to take stock. Years of neglect had taken their toll on the body and ruined the fine physique he was once proud of. So he decided to rebuild his body. Charles wasn't content to lose a few kilos and become a little fitter; he was determined to turn his flab back into muscle mass and regain the fitness he had decades ago.

Soon after, Charles marched into a gym to consult with a champion body-builder. The trainer looked down at him.

"You want what?"

"I want a beach body," Charles repeated.

"A beach body...." The trainer pursed his lips. "How old are you, sir?"

"87."

Silence.

"Get undressed," the trainer said.

After inspecting the sagging, weathered body, the trainer rolled his eyes. "It won't be easy," he said. "I'll work with you but only if you follow my advice to the letter."

Charles agreed to the trainer's conditions and started working out. Slowly, his body lost fat, gained muscle, and became more flexible. His fitness increased, and his mood improved.

He later wrote, "I may not have known it as I set out to reinvent myself, but my best years were ahead of me."

A few years later, Charles Eugster became a bodybuilding champion and went on to become a phenomenal athlete. In his 80s and 90s, he became the World Masters Rowing Champion, the European Decathlon Champion, the Swiss National Fitness Champion, and a Masters Bodybuilding Champion.

However, at 95, he was forced to give up rowing because of a heart murmur. In his book, *Age is Just a Number*, he wrote, "No doubt on that day many people assumed I would shuffle off into the sunset and reflect on my former glories. Without question, it was a painful and sad moment in my life, but I had amassed enough experience over the years to know that for every door that closes, another cracks open and a bright light shines through."

His research into the best exercise patterns for older people showed that bursts of strenuous exercise are better than endurance training and that HIIT (high-intensity interval training) is good for heart health. Charles met with his new performance trainer, Sylvia Gattiker, and shared his idea for a new direction.

"Running?" Sylvia said, taken aback.

"*Sprinting!*" Charles exclaimed. "Fast and furious!"

That was when Charles decided to reinvent himself once again. He took up sprinting and other disciplines of track and field. Within two years, Charles Eugster became a champion sprinter for his age group. At 96, he blitzed the "Over-95 200 Meter" World Record. With that record, Charles Eugster became the greatest athlete ever over 90!

But his athletic achievements were only one aspect of this *youthful ager*. Charles continued to work, once he got his life back on track after his wife's death. At 90, he was approached by a European chain of gyms to travel around and give talks. As a result, he became an accomplished public speaker, even giving a TED talk.

Charles was always on a crusade to change people's ideas of retirement. He said, "I personally think that retirement is one of the worst things that's ever been designed by mankind. It's a financial disaster and a health catastrophe." He was adamant that work in its many forms—whether as a volunteer, an employee, a creative, or an entrepreneur—is essential for a fulfilling life.

At age 97, Charles Eugster proclaimed, "Old age, as I've experienced it, is one of the most fantastic periods of life. It's absolutely marvelous; it's stupendous, it's terrific, amazing, exciting, glorious!"

I think one of the secrets of Charles's golden years lay in his vision of the future. Ask most people over 70 what their goals are, and you won't get much of a response. When Charles Eugster was asked at 96 how he saw his future, this was his answer:

"I want to change the world. I'm writing a book called *Age is Just a Number*, which I hope to publish this year. Then I want to establish fitness centers for those over 70 and start a job creation company to retrain older people. Then, of course, I want to have some connection with nutrition for the old. And the other thing in the back of my mind is that I would like to create a fashion label for older people."

As you can see, Charles Eugster wasn't going to run out of projects any time soon! His inspiring book, called *Age is Just a Number,* was published in January 2017. With this, he became the oldest first-time author at the age of 97.

Reflection

The turning point in Charles Eugster's life came when he caught sight of himself in the mirror and realized that he was out of shape.

His life story shows that it's never too old to get back in shape. The body is extremely responsive, and even small, positive changes to your lifestyle can have significant results. However, you need to set clearly defined goals for the changes you want to see in the future.

> *"If you don't know where you're going,*
> *any road will get you there."*
> ~Lewis Carroll

Establishing an exercise routine can seem like a daunting task. The problem of starting new, positive habits is that whenever you initiate change, you give yourself a fright. In her book *This Year I Will*, M. J. Ryan explains, "Whenever we initiate change, even a positive one, we activate fear in our emotional brain....If the fear is big enough, the fight-or-flight response will go off and we'll run from what we're trying to do."

That's why it's good to get back in shape very gradually by using the strategy of continuous, incremental change.

No matter where you are right now, the truth is that you can turn your life around at any age. All you need is a deep desire for change. And that change doesn't have to mean aiming to become an athlete!

> *"Recognizing that you are not where you want to*
> *be is a starting point to begin changing your life."*
> ~Deborah Day

3 If You Attempt the Impossible

The 61-year-old farmer showed up in overalls and work boots. Instead of lycra, he was wearing long pants with holes cut for ventilation. A hush fell when Cliff went to the registration desk and picked up a race number.

"You gonna race?" one of the competitors called out.

"Yep," Cliff said.

"In your boots?" the guy continued. People in the crowd chuckled.

Then, a reporter asked him if he thought he could win. "Yep. I'll give it a go," Cliff said. He was willing to try anything!

Cliff Young had lined up for one of the world's most grueling endurance races, the Sydney to Melbourne ultra-marathon which stretches over 875 kilometers.

When the starter gun sounded, the field of fit, young guys breezed past him. The crowd laughed out loud when they saw that Cliff couldn't run properly. He seemed to shuffle along at a snail's pace.

In this race, competitors would usually complete the course over five days, running about eighteen hours a day and sleeping for the remaining six.

But nobody told Cliff about this. When his competitors woke up after the first night, they asked how the "old looney" was doing. "Oh, he's doing good," one of the organizers said. "He ran all night and is two hours ahead of you guys." As you can imagine, this wiped the smile off their faces.

Cliff kept on running with minimal stops, lengthening the lead each day. During the first few days, he fell and injured his shoulder. But Cliff soldiered on.

Cliff's training had consisted of herding livestock on his farm. "I grew up on a farm where we couldn't afford horses or four-wheel drives. Whenever the storms would roll in, I'd have to go out and round up the sheep. Sometimes I would have to run those sheep for two or three days. It took a long time, but I'd catch them."

His performance-enhancing diet consisted of Weet-Bix, cold tinned spaghetti, boiled potatoes, egg flips, and pumpkin.

Halfway through the race, the weather turned bad and it started to bucket down. Someone tried to hand Cliff a water-proof jacket, but his shoulder was causing him so much pain that he couldn't lift his arm to put it on. Finally, Coleman, the race director, caught up with Cliff and suggested he should have a pain-killing injection in his shoulder. "He told me where I could stick my needle in no uncertain terms," Coleman recalled. "Then he just plodded on."

Cliff's support crew, Wally and Wobbles, were earthy types, just like Cliff. Wobbles got his name from having a lopsided walk after a bout of polio as a child.

Apparently, on their way to catch up with Cliff, just outside the town of Tumblong, Wally and Wobbles were about to pass the race's youngest competitor, John Connellan, when they realized he was struggling.

Wally leant out of the clapped-out van. "Hey, what's up with you, mate?" he yelled, trying to be heard above the rattle of the engine.

"Aaw, Wally, damn, my ankles are swollen, my back hurts, my legs ache ..."

"Listen, mate," Wally replied. "You ain't tired till your eyes bleed! Now, get on with it!"

But the encouragement was to no avail. At the next town, Connellan slumped into a chair, grabbed a beer, and said to the reporters, "Why doesn't somebody shoot that little bloke out in front? I just can't believe that a 61-year-old is making mincemeat of us all."

Every day of the race, Cliff began to forge further ahead, getting by on only a few hours' sleep each night. Finally, Cliff Young won the race, running 875 km in five days, 14 hours and 35 minutes—the equivalent of almost four marathons a day. He shattered the previous race record by more than two days!

Cliff Young earned the event's $10,000 grand prize. Cliff didn't feel he needed more money than the modest $2,000 a year he earned, so he shared the prize money with other competitors and his support crew. But the excitement and the tiredness got to him. Apparently, his legs gave out after the presentation of the prize and he had to be carried off the stage.

The Australian sports journalist Neil Kearney wrote, "He was an unspoiled character, pure in his way. He was good with people, he was charming, self-deprecating and the little Aussie battler. He was a guy no one expected to win. And this was a phenomenal challenge, that distance down the highway, the relentless nature of it, the fact that it broke good men, proven men who'd run all around the world."

Cliff Young left Sydney as a nobody and arrived in Melbourne as Australia's most improbable national hero. His gait, the *Young Shuffle*, was later adopted by some ultra runners because it saves energy over long distances.

After his race, he advised others in the style of Forrest Gump:

"Get out of your wheelchairs and start doing a few laps, if you can. If you don't get any exercise your joints start seizing up like a rusty engine. It is like rust that gets into a vehicle. I reckon you have to keep your joints moving. Absolutely. No matter what you do, you have to keep moving. If you don't wear out, you rust out, and you rust out quicker than you wear out."

Cliff, the *youthful ager,* was willing to try anything, even if others thought his goals were impossible to achieve. At 76, Cliff hit the headlines once again when he attempted to run around Australia's 16,000 kilometer border to raise money for homeless children. Cliff completed 6,520 kilometers and was raring to continue. However, the support guy in the dodgy van had a heart attack so, reluctantly, Cliff had to stop the project.

If an Australian farmer in his 60s and 70s was willing to try anything and overcame seemingly impossible challenges, imagine what you could achieve.

Reflection

What are your dreams? What mental, physical, or creative goals do you want to achieve?

There are three steps to make your dreams become a reality like Cliff Young did. The first step is to pick a goal you truly want to achieve. The second step is to determine the smallest action which will move you toward your goal. And the third step is to schedule the date when you will take action.

It's important not to share your dreams with naysayers. Many people like to kill the dreams of others because they feel threatened by seeing someone aim high. That's why it's important to surround yourself with people who have a positive attitude and will support you in reaching your dreams.

> "Keep away from people who try to belittle your ambitions. Small people do that, but the really great make you feel that you, too, can somehow become great"
> ~Mark Twain

4 The Astonishing Outcome of Persistence

*A*nna Mary Robertson, a farmer's wife in rural America, was 67 when here husband died. After his death, her youngest son managed the farm and Anna took up embroidery to fill the void in her life.

So far, there's nothing that would make you think that Anna's life was going to become to one of the most inspiring stories of *youthful aging*, right?

Anna loved embroidery. She enjoyed creating country scenes with the flat patterns of cross-stitching. However, at 78, her hands became too crippled by arthritis to continue her hobby. One day, she was wallpapering her parlor and ran out of paper. To finish, she put up a fireboard and painted a scene. That's when Anna decided to switch to painting. She couldn't hold a needle, but she could grip a brush, and she had been too busy all her life to be idle.

She later said, "I painted for pleasure, to keep busy and to pass the time away."

Anna decided to paint every day without fail, and her hoard of pictures gradually grew. To get rid of her growing stack of painted boards, her family persuaded her to show them—along with some raspberry jam and strawberry preserves—at a nearby country fair. Her jam won a ribbon, but nobody took notice of her paintings. However, a drugstore in nearby Hoosick Falls later agreed to display them in their window.

For years, Anna's paintings sat in the store window, gathering dust. They were displayed alongside knitted booties, cross-stitch samplers, babies' bonnets, and other handiwork created by local homemakers.

Then, one day, her life changed forever.

Louis J. Caldor, a New York art collector who was driving through Hoosick Falls, saw her paintings in the shop window and slammed on the brakes. He rushed in, shouting, "Who is this artist?" The shopgirl stuttered as she told him Anna's name and Caldor immediately bought all the pictures in the window.

He then dashed to the family farm and bought ten more pictures from Anna. Looking her in the eye, he said, "I will make you famous!" Anna was taken aback, and her daughters thought the man was crazy.

Caldor took his trove of paintings to New York and made the rounds of galleries and museums, trying to interest them in Anna's work. But nobody wanted to show her pictures. When dealers and curators found out she was 78, they backed off, fearing she wouldn't live long enough for them to recoup the cost of staging a show.

However, in the next year, Caldor managed to get her an invitation to an exhibition of "contemporary unknown painters" at the Museum of Modern Art in New York where three of her pictures elicited only a meager response.

Caldor could not get a gallery to show her work. Undeterred, he kept on asking around. Finally, he showed Anna's pictures to the Vietnamese immigrant Otto Kallir who had just opened a new gallery in Manhattan, called "St. Etienne." Kallir fell in love with Anna Mary's paintings, believing that the work of self-taught artists is more original than that of trained painters. Soon, Otto Kallir put Anna under contract for her first big show. She was 80 years old at the time.

Her paintings of homely farm life and rural countrysides were an instant success. People loved the sense of nostalgia they evoked. Otto Kallir had given the exhibition the muted title "What a Farmwife Painted." However, a journalist came upon her local nickname, and that is how she became known as "Grandma Moses."

Grandma Moses soon became a superstar and took her place as one of the most treasured American artists.

Journalists of the time described her as "cheerful as a cricket" with "mischievous gray eyes and a quick wit." She was evidently a spirited woman with an indomitable spirit.

"I'll get an inspiration and start painting," Grandma Moses said. "Then I'll forget everything, everything except how things used to be and how to paint it so people will know how we used to live." She always painted from the top down: "First the sky, then the mountains, then the hills, then the trees, then the houses, then the cattle and then the people."

In a television interview on CBS News, correspondent Edward R. Murrow asked Anna about learning to paint.

"What sort of advice would you give to those people if they had time to try their hand at painting?"

"Well, anybody can paint that wants to paint," Grandma Moses replied.

"Can they?"

Grandma Moses smiled. "Oh sure. Anybody can paint."

She created over a thousand paintings of rural life in America, twenty-five of them after she had passed her 100th birthday. Her depictions of times gone by became famous all over the world. Asked what she thought of being labeled a "primitive artist," she quipped, "A primitive artist is an amateur whose work sells."

Reproductions of her work still fly off the shelves, and by 2018, an estimated 50 million Grandma Moses Christmas cards had been sold in the U.S.

Grandma Moses's life is a splendid example of *youthful aging.*

She followed her calling and felt compelled to paint, no matter what others thought of her paintings.

You can be sure she had bad days and good days like everyone else. Nevertheless, she persisted. Grandma Moses painted every day without fail, often spending five hours or more, propped up by cushions and sitting on a battered swivel chair, while the board she painted on rested atop an old kitchen table.

In her last year, she said, "I look back on my life like a good day's work, it was done, and I feel satisfied with it. I was happy and contented, I knew nothing better and made the best out of what life offered. And life is what we make it, always has been, always will be."

Reflection

Grandma Moses showed the world that it's never too late to bloom and prosper.

However, success doesn't happen if you just sit around and wait for it; you need to meet good fortune halfway. Grandma Moses's secret of success was the tenacity with which she developed her talent.

Imagine a skill you would like to develop. What would it be?

Once you know which skill you are drawn to, consider how you could develop it. As you can see from Grandma Moses's story, the key to mastery is practicing your chosen skill daily.

Would you be willing to devote five minutes a day to your chosen skill?

You may think five minutes is not enough time to have any impact. However, even just a few moments to scribble words in your notebook, sketch something on paper, read a page of an informative book, play a piece of music, or complete a few physical exercises will build skills and accumulate knowledge and experience as time goes by.

5 To Stay Forever Young

When two young roommates, Bob Cilman and Bill Newman, had a conversation about their dreams of the future, Cilman came up with a weird idea. Instead of wanting to become a successful lawyer, like Bill, Bob talked about his idea of starting a singing group of seniors who would perform rock'n roll, punk, and soul songs.

"What do you think?" Cilman asked.

"Bad idea," Newman replied.

At the time, Cilman had found work at the Walter Salvo House in Northampton, dishing out food to the elderly residents. Bob had taken the job because it came with health insurance. One evening, fellow worker Judith Sharpe came to Bob and suggested a piano might be a good thing for the house.

Once they got a piano, Cilman thought a sing-along might be fun for the residents. "I put out a call to see if anyone wanted to sing, and twenty-five people showed up," he said.

Little did Bob know that the first sing-along in the Walter Salvo House would start a revolution. That's how the Young@Heart Chorus, the choir with an average age of 81, began.

Cilman later said, "Some ideas you just don't pass by Bill Newman first."

A year later, the group was ready for their first performance. In their early years, the choral group became known locally for their collaborations with breakdancers from a local housing project, Cambodian folk musicians, the Pioneer Valley Gay Men's Chorus and Roy Faudree's experimental "No Theater". Bob Cilman soon started to experiment with rock songs.

Group member Fred Knittle said, "We never heard some of these songs before. My attitude was: 'Turn it down and turn it off.' The Clash? We wouldn't have allowed that in our house. Sonic Youth? No way, shape or form." That was before he started to enjoy learning and performing rock, punk, and other modern pop music songs. Steve Martin, an ex-Marine, said, "I was learning a whole new type of music. It was as if someone had opened a door."

For Steve, 82 years old, the door opened to a vibrant, exciting, and satisfying new chapter of life.

Bob Cilman is a demanding Chorus Master. He said, "I work them hard. This is not a social service. I'm working with people to create something that's really worth seeing."

The turning point came when the Young@Heart Chorus performed with the No Theater at the Rotterdam Festival in 1996. Cilman recalled, "The first time, they could only get 90 people to see it. But the next night we sold out all 250 seats. We were brought back with that show twice a year to Europe for the next eight years."

Touring created some new challenges. In an interview[1] with Eleanor Yap, Cilman said, "The first time we traveled, it was such a scary proposition. Everything went fine, but we were nervous about this new kind of travel. We actually brought a doctor with us, and he was the only one who got sick!"

When they performed their show "Road to Nowhere" in London, Sally George, a documentary filmmaker, dragged her husband, Stephen, along to see Young@Heart. Stephen Hall later said, "I wasn't sure what we were dealing with. Was this kind of a dancing bear territory? ...I did know they had great reviews, and that was one of the things that convinced me to go, but I wasn't sure what I was going to see. Was it going to be some sort of karaoke? I went to London and the music struck me as being really exciting."

At the time, Stephen Hall and Sally George were planning to do a film about aging and they thought a film about the Chorus would work well. This led to creating the award-winning documentary film *Young@Heart*.

This film has many poignant moments—like the one where the Chorus sings Bob Dylan's "Forever Young" to a group of prisoners. You can see even some of the most hardened inmates moved to tears. This concert was part of the Prison Project, a way to cultivate a relationship between the Chorus and members of local prison populations through rehearsals in prison.

After their first concert in prison, Bob Cilman thought it would be a great idea to sing together. He found some keen singers among the prisoners, and soon inmates clamored to be allowed to sing with the Chorus in their prison concerts.

Some singers even joined the Chorus in public shows, once they had been shifted to minimum-security prisons and were given leave.

---

[1] http://www.agelessonline.net/2143/stage-presence/

Prison Deputy Superintendent Melinda Cady said, "The Young@Heart Chorus gives these guys an opportunity to see themselves in different roles, as members of something good."

After his first rehearsal, one of the prisoners was interviewed by a reporter. "Nelson, you have a great voice," the reporter said. "When did you start singing?"

"At 9:30."

"I mean in your life."

"That's it. At 9:30," Nelson said.

A story making the rounds is that one of the prisoners enjoyed singing with the Chorus so much, he even broke out of jail to see Young@Heart in concert!

Since the film aired, many have applied to join the Chorus. To be considered for Young@Heart, people have to be at least 73 years old and have to commit to a strenuous touring schedule, as well as help with the Prison Project.

Members want to inspire their audience. Steve Martin said, "I hope people watching us will get off the couch and do something with their life. Don't quit in life! Be active; be something."

"When we come out and do some of these jumping songs, they're just amazed," Jack Schnepp said of people in the audience. "They say, 'Gee, I wish I could do that.' And what we're trying to do is tell them, 'You can. Just get out here and do it!'"

"May your heart always be joyful,
May your song always be sung.
And may you stay
Forever young."
~Bob Dylan

Reflection

When choir member Steve Martin said, "I hope people watching us will get off the couch and do something with their life. Don't quit in life! Be active; be something," he was talking to us all.

Taking action isn't that difficult. But isolated actions don't add up to a transformation of life. Becoming a *youthful ager* is a personal revolution that awakens the greatness within you. This revolution begins with taking stock of your current development.

Take a look at the following five dimensions of life and consider whether you are developing in these areas.

1. Physical development: are you working on getting your body and health into better shape?

2. Mental development: are you stimulating your mind and creativity and working on a positive attitude?

3. Occupational development: are you developing new skills and taking opportunities for paid, creative, or voluntary work?

4. Social development: are you establishing and maintaining positive relationships with others?

5. Spiritual development: are you finding meaning in your life and practicing mindfulness, meditation, or prayer?

6. Remember, it's never too late to start your journey of self-development.

"Asking the proper questions is the central action of transformation. Questions are the key that causes the secret doors of the psyche to swing open."
~Clarissa Pinkola Estes

6 The Untapped Potential of Optimism

> "There's nothing in a caterpillar that tells you it's going to be a butterfly. Who knows what a person can become?"
> ~Buckminster Fuller

How do you want to spend the rest of your life?

The journalist Roy Rowan, born in 1920, faced this question after retiring. Like many people, he initially felt at a loss when contemplating life without his job.

When Roy had worked as a foreign correspondent, he experienced many dangerous situations, like the time he was evacuated on the last day of the fall of Saigon. With a small group of other correspondents and photographers, he ended up at the airport, under Marine guard, waiting for the helicopters to be ready.

Roy later wrote, "Just as our group of fifty prepared to leave...the Marine at the door shouted, 'No baggage!' Suitcases and bags were ripped open as evacuees fished for their passports, papers and other valuables. I said goodbye to my faithful Olivetti, grabbed my tape recorder and camera and got ready to run like hell. The door opened. Outside I could see helmeted, flak-jacketed Marines—lots of them—crouched against the building, their M16s, grenade launchers, and mortars all at the ready."

You might wonder how someone with such an exciting job was able to transition to a fulfilling life after retirement. However, Roy pivoted to become a best-selling author and managed to create a vibrant and productive life in his mature years. The key to his success was his optimism and his belief that it's never too late to keep doing what you love.

Roy Rowan even credited his positive outlook with beating melanoma from which his doctors had only given him a fifty percent chance of recovery when he was 54.

In his book *Never Too Late,* published in 2012 when Roy was 92, he describes remaining standing when people offered him a seat on a bus. His reason was, "…Not just to show that I'm still steady on my feet, but to stand up for old age as a vibrant and productive time of life." This attitude reminds me of my mother, Joan S. Jaksch. Well into her 80s, she would give up her seat on the bus to people decades younger.

Roy Rowan's daily routine was impressive. In his 90s, he would get up at 5 AM, write, work out, eat breakfast, write some more until it was time for a late lunch, and then go for an afternoon walk. In the summertime, surf casting was his favorite pastime. His goal was "to keep on doing the same things that motivated me in my younger years—some that generate a sense of accomplishment, others that simply provide relaxation or pleasure."

Roy loved the following quote from Alexander Calder, the artist famous for his huge metal sculptures. Calder was asked, "Now that you're older, how to you handle these heavy pieces of steel?"

"With elation," he shot back.

Roy counted Pablo Picasso and Pablo Casals among his heroes because both the artist and the cellist produced masterpieces well into their 90s.

Casals is also one of my heroes because I had the good fortune to hear him play. When I was 19 years old, I traveled from Germany to Prades, an ancient village nestling in the shadow of Mont Canigou in the Catalan Pyrenees. I had heard that Master Pablo Casals was going to perform in the festival he had organized.

At the time, I couldn't imagine how a 90-year-old could still play an instrument. After all, I was still a teenager and thought that being "old" starts at 35!

When I entered the ancient church of St. Pierre, which served as the concert hall, my eye was drawn to the gleaming golden altarpiece. Everything else lay in darkness. I looked around. Beside me, some people were kneeling in prayer, others were talking in hushed tones, all of us waiting for the concert to begin. Then a bell rang and an usher announced that there should be no applause.

When the spotlights came on, Casals appeared in front of the altar: a small, plump man with a burnished bald head and an ageless face. A sigh went up in the audience. I sat on the edge of my seat waiting for Bach's Suite in D minor for solo violoncello to begin.

When the first, perfect phrase floated through the church, I disappeared into the music, soaring and dipping with the exquisite sounds like an eagle flying over ancient landscapes.

After the concert, the audience gathered in the plaza outside the church, waiting for Casals to appear. When the master emerged on the arm of his beautiful wife, the crowd surged toward him, shouting and clapping. One woman clasped her hands, saying, "I did not know such music could exist this side of heaven."

Over 50 years after the event, I am still in awe of Casal's transcendent mastery where self and instrument are forgotten in the act of playing.

This kind of mastery only happens when we pour a whole, long life into our activities. No wonder Roy Rowan counted Casals as one of his heroes! As a writer, Rowan aspired to a supreme mastery of his craft—and he achieved his goal.

After retirement, Roy wrote three memoirs: *Powerful People: From Mao to Now, A Reporter's Fifty-Year Pursuit, Chasing the Dragon: A Veteran Journalist's Firsthand Account of the 1946-1949 Chinese Revolution* and his last book, *Never Too Late: A 90-Year-Old's Pursuit Of A Whirlwind Life.* These were far from his only literary works. He called becoming an author his "second career'"

Roy pointed out in his book *Never Too Late*, "Launching a second career takes what I call the 3 Es: Enthusiasm to try something new, Exertion to get started, and the Energy not to quit."

Whether you choose to recycle old hobbies, acquire a new skill, or take up volunteer work, there are endless possibilities. You could learn a new language, or play a musical instrument, or take up carpentry, weaving or other handicrafts. You could study astronomy, or any other area of expertise that strikes your fancy. If you want to take up academic study, all you need is Internet access, as many universities offer free courses on Coursera[2]or with other online course providers.

---

[2] https://coursera.com

If you doubt you have a talent worth developing, heed what the inventor Buckminster Fuller said: "There's nothing in a caterpillar that tells you it's going to be a butterfly. Who knows what a person can become?"

Roy's tip for *youthful aging* is to cultivate an optimistic state of mind because it will make you feel engaged, hopeful, and happy. He said about optimism, "It not only determines your own outlook, but affects how others react to you, as negative and positive attitudes are both rabidly contagious." Roy encouraged us to "…stand up for old age as a vibrant and productive time of life."

Like Roy, we can all find our "second career," our *raison d'etre*, by revving up an inner passion and being optimistic.

The second half of life can hold even greater promise than the first.

Reflection

We can learn the value of optimism from Roy Rowan.

Science supports the importance of having a positive attitude. Psychologists from the Netherlands interviewed over a thousand men and women between the ages of 65 and 85. Researchers found that those participants who had reported higher levels of optimism were 55 percent less likely to die during the nine-year follow-up period from any cause as compared to the pessimistic group.

How optimistic are you? Find out by answering the following two questions:

1. Do you often feel like life is full of promise?

2. Do you still have many goals to strive for?

If you can't find much positivity within, consider this ancient Cherokee parable.

One evening, an old Cherokee told his grandson about a battle that goes on inside people.

He said, "My son, there is a battle between two 'wolves' inside of us. One is evil. It is anger, envy, jealousy, sorrow, regret, greed, and arrogance.

The other is good. It is joy, peace, love, hope, serenity, humility, and kindness."

The grandson thought about this for a minute and then asked: "Which wolf wins?"

The old Cherokee replied, "The one you feed."

Which of the two "wolves" do you feed?

You can train your mind to stop going down negative paths. Notice your pessimistic thoughts and rephrase them so that you create new, positive neural pathways in your brain.

The Mysterious Power of Mind over Body

*I*magine a woman fracturing her pelvis and a femur in her mid-80s. She would most likely end up with a walker or in a wheelchair, right?

Hurtling downhill on her bike at age 84, Sister Madonna Buder was swiped by a car and ended up with severe injuries, including a busted pelvis.

Her doctors expected her to end up disabled, but Sister Buder, the *Iron Nun,* had a different agenda. Her focus was to get back to racing as quickly as possible.

She immediately began an exercise regimen of water jogging and working out on an elliptical trainer—against her doctor's orders.

Just three months later, she entered the Ironman triathlon in Cambridge, Maryland, to complete the 2.4-mile swim, 112-mile bike and 26.2-mile run alongside some of the best in the world. Afterward, she said the run was "laboring" because of her injury, but the bike ride went smoothly. Later the same year, the Iron Nun competed at the world championship Ironman in Hawaii—at age 84.

Why was Madonna Buder able to recover fast and train her way back to extreme fitness when many people her age would expect to remain disabled for the rest of their life? Let's take a look at the Iron Nun's life to discover her secret.

Sister Madonna Buder was born in St. Louis, Missouri, in 1930. As a teenager, she became an accomplished horsewoman, winning many equestrian tournaments. In her book *The Grace to Race*, she talks about her time as a youngster:

"My life was filled with adventures and near misses: capsized sailboats, sledding mishaps, mountaineering ordeals, crashes on roller skates."

The marriage of her parents was a balancing of opposites. Her father was of German origin and his adventurous, realistic, and practical outlook left his mark on his daughter. In contrast, Madonna inherited her creative and spiritual strengths from her mother who was of French descent.

Madonna grew up a tomboy. She hated the ballet lessons she was forced to go to and dreamed of playing outside when she had to practice the piano. When necessary, she stepped forward to protect her younger brothers, as she explained in *The Grace to Race:*

"When the neighborhood bullies threatened to interrupt our gang at play, I suggested we beat it to the back porch and lock ourselves inside. But my brother didn't move fast enough, and the two bullies grabbed him. I bolted out of the front door of our neighbor's house and surprised my brother's captors by yelling, 'Let my brother go!' I doubled my fist and planted it squarely in the oldest boy's left eye, and, as the assailant winced from the blow, I pulled my brother out of his grip. After that, we were no longer bothered."

Growing up, Madonna Buder developed a strong spiritual side and finally decided—even though she was courted by some attractive young men—to enter an order and be ordained as a nun. You can imagine that it was not without a struggle for this carefree spirit to submit to the discipline of an order.

More than two decades after joining the order, a strange kind of freedom beckoned at last.

When Sister Buder was 48, a priest talked to her about taking up exercise. He suggested running along the beach because, as he explained, running harmonizes mind, body, and soul. Following his advice, she started jogging on the sand. To her surprise, running was a joyful release.

"Once I began running, I rediscovered my adventurous spirit."

Soon, Madonna started competing in races. Then, she discovered triathlons and took to them with a passion that raised eyebrows in her religious community. As one of the sisters said, "You are such a free spirit, we don't know how to contain you."

Luckily, Sister Madonna found a way to transfer to a less restrictive order that allowed her to take responsibility for her life: "You are responsible for yourself; you're no longer in an ivory castle being protected. You're out with the rest of the people earning your own living, doing your own apostolic work."

When she first started training for a race to raise money for charity, her body complained. She later wrote, "My calves were so tight, I couldn't even push them in, and my knees were so swollen I could hardly bend them…I burst out in tears, thinking 'God, I can't do this. I know I promised, but my body isn't going to let me!'"

Most people would have given up after such a painful start, but Sister Madonna isn't one to give up easily: "I tend to attack everything with determination and exert every fiber of my being once I am committed to a goal."

Once she had won a few races, Madonna Buder heard about triathlons.

"I was introduced to triathlons through another runner who had just come back from doing the Hawaiian Ironman. And he said, 'Sister, you have got to try this.' He told me the distances, and I was repulsed by the whole idea. I hadn't swum for years; I just did it as a kid. And I'm not in favor of going in with a bunch of people and their flailing arms and legs and getting smashed. I didn't own a bike."

Three years later, Sister Madonna completed her first triathlon.

When she was 76, she became the oldest woman to complete the Ironman triathlon, a record she broke every year after that. To date, the *Iron Nun* has completed over 340 triathlons—including 46 Ironman events—and is a Senior Olympian with several records in various distances. In all of her time as a top athlete, she has held to three principles: "Don't waste time training for training's sake, incorporate the workout into your daily life by using the day's demands to challenge yourself physically, and make training joyful."

The key to Sister Madonna's success is using her mind to tune her body.

She said, "Your mind, your thoughts control who you are. So it's very important to watch what you think because your thoughts become a part of you."

In my experience, our bodies have tremendous untapped potential.

In 2018, I took up CrossFit training as an experiment to see how a 70-year-old body would respond to a sharp uptick in exercise intensity. As you may know, CrossFit is one of the hardest training systems.

I was apprehensive when I went to my initial training sessions as the workouts were extremely challenging. They included gymnastics, cardio exercises, and olympic weight lifting—which I had never done before.

Six weeks into training, Zoe, a young CrossFit student, approached me.

"Hey Mary, why don't you join us for the Master's League? We're going to meet up on Saturdays and do some special workouts. It'll be fun!"

"Oh," I said. "That's sound nice. I'll come along."

I signed up without reading the fine print. Later, I was shocked to find out I had entered an International CrossFit Competition!

The top age bracket was 60+ and I was competing with women in New Zealand and Australia who were ten years younger. In the following weeks, I had to complete four hair-raising competition workouts that were supervised and signed off on by a trainer.

I ended up as number 5 in New Zealand and placed number 2 in the South Island of New Zealand. If you had asked me at the start of my CrossFit training whether I could imagine competing in an international competition after only two months of training, I would have laughed outright. Luckily, I was game to try it and my body rose to the challenge.

I was amazed to see how quickly my fitness and strength picked up. Even though I trained hard, I never had the slightest injury and felt vitally alive. To inspire others, I documented my CrossFit experiment on Youtube. CrossFit has taken me from being a reasonably fit person to being an athlete. I am continuing to train both in karate, as well as CrossFit, as I want to hone my skills and boost my fitness even more.

This experience taught me that we can push our bodies to great lengths, and that body and mind respond with a healthy glow if we step up to challenges.

"The only failure is not to try;
your effort in itself is a success."
~Sister Madonna Buder

Reflection

Sister Madonna Buder became a successful athlete because she believed in the ability of her body to evolve.

As psychologist Professor Ellen J. Langer says in her book *Mindfulness*, "It is not primarily our physical selves that limit us but rather our mindset about our physical limits."

A mindset is a habit of the mind. It is a belief, attitude and assumption we create about who we are and how the world works. The good news is that we can change our mindsets; they are not written in stone.

It's especially important for your health and wellbeing that you have a positive mindset about your body. Our bodies are capable of so much more than we envisage! To understand your habit of the mind, reflect on the question below.

What is your mindset about physical limitations?

> *"Your beliefs become your thoughts, your thoughts become your words, your words become your actions, your actions become your habits, your habits become your values, your values become your destiny."*
> ~Mahatma Gandhi

8 Scandal, Murder, and the Rebirth of a Career

*A*t retirement age, he was a washout. His colleagues in the field of architecture looked down on him as a "has-been." His style was deemed old-fashioned, and hardly anyone was willing to commission a design.

Architect Frank Lloyd Wright was first celebrated, then ridiculed, and then forgotten. He had broken all the rules in his art and his life. He was notorious and unpredictable. And, at 65, he was broke.

He had inherited from his father an inability to live within his means. Wright used to say, "As long as we have the luxuries, the necessities will look after themselves."

With no money, no prospects, a staff of draftsmen to pay, a farm to run, and a new wife and a little daughter to support, Frank's retirement years threatened to be a disaster.

But Wright had a secret weapon in life: his vitality. He was, as one of his draftsmen remembered, "Two hundred percent alive."

Even though most people had written him off, Frank Lloyd Wright believed in himself. Wright said, "I think that any man who really has faith in himself will be dubbed arrogant by his fellows."

His brash confidence was not the only thing that irritated his contemporaries. His love life also had tongues wagging. At first, when he was in his 20s, he seemed willing to accept the conventions of society. He married a young, well-bred girl called Kitty, and they had six children.

By the time he was 40, Wright had everything an architect could wish for: a successful career, a beautiful home, and a loving wife and family. However, this comfortable life felt like a trap, and his creativity suffered. He later said about this time, "I was losing my grip on work, even my interest in it. I could see no way out."

At the time, the Wrights lived close to a couple, called Edwin and Mamah Cheney, who were Frank's clients. Mamah was spirited and artistic, an early feminist who was sick of the traditional role of wife and mother.

Frank fell in love with Mamah, and they started a clandestine affair. When Kitty found out, she refused to give Frank a divorce because she hoped this fling would burn itself out. But a year later, Wright abruptly closed his studio, left his wife and six children, and ran off to Europe with Mamah. All Wright left behind was unpaid bills.

The conservative society of Chicago was shocked by the scandal, and newspaper reporters followed the pair to Europe, hoping for salacious tidbits. Frank and Mamah stayed in Europe for a year in what Wright called "voluntary exile."

When the scandal died down, the pair returned to America, and Wright built a mansion for himself and his mistress in Wisconsin, called Taliesin.

The pair lived at Taliesin for three happy years. Mamah wrote, ran the household, and enjoyed occasional visits from her children. But this idyllic life was soon to be shattered by tragedy.

Wright had landed a big commission for the Midway Gardens, a whole block in Chicago that he was to transform into a pleasure garden. Together with his son, John, now his assistant, Wright immersed himself in this project, returning to Taliesin regularly to be with Mamah.

But Frank's world was suddenly devastated.

News of the disaster came as his son John—who was supervising the work at Midway Gardens—was having lunch on a scaffold, while his father was standing at the drawing board. The office secretary came to say that Mr. Wright senior was wanted on the telephone. John soon became aware of an eerie silence, broken only by his father's labored breathing and a groan. John spun around. Frank Wright was clinging to the table for support, his face ashen.

A few months previously, Wright had hired as a butler a West Indian man called Julian Carleton. On the day of the tragedy, wearing his white dinner jacket, Julian served lunch for Mamah and her two young children who had come for a summer visit.

While Mamah, her children, and the workmen were eating lunch, Carleton quietly bolted all the windows and doors, except one. He went outside and poured gasoline all around the house. Then he lit a match. Within seconds, the house was engulfed in flames.

People tried to escape, but Julian stood outside, brandishing an ax. It was a horrific scene. Everyone screamed. Some of the draftsmen were on fire, rolling on the ground. With a blow to her head, Julian killed Mamah, then her two children, and finally the workmen. At the end of the attack, seven people lay dead, and Taliesin was a smoldering ruin.

On receiving the news, Frank and his son traveled to Taliesin. Beside himself with grief, Wright forbade the undertakers to touch Mamah's body and made a simple pine box for a coffin. He filled it with flowers and his son and cousins helped him bury her in a small cemetery.

Frank was distraught, but found consolation in his work. "There is release from anguish in action," he later explained. He doggedly began to rebuild Taliesin on the ashes of the doomed house.

A year later, on the rebound, Frank married Miriam Noel. It didn't go well. She was an unstable and dangerous morphine addict who threatened him with a knife before she stormed out of the house.

Frank wasn't alone for long. In a chance encounter at the opera, he met Olgivanna, then in her 20s. He invited her to Taliesin and soon she was pregnant with his child. Once again, Frank was the focus of scandal. The papers had plenty to write about because Miriam broke into the house and threatened to shoot the couple. Wright's few clients turned away in disgust at the scandal.

When Wright was 67, his career lay in ruins. But he stubbornly refused to admit defeat. Following a suggestion by Olgivanna, he wrote his autobiography. This alerted younger architects to his work.

Then he started the Taliesin Fellowship through which young architects could learn by living and working side-by-side with the master. The idea caught on, a stream of young architects descended upon Taliesin, and Wright was in funds again. But to the outside world, he was finished.

At the time, Wright was eclipsed by the "International Style" of Mies van der Rohe and Walter Gropius. Then, when Wright was 69, a department store owner asked him to create a holiday home for his family, close to their favorite waterfall. Wright created a stunning design and called the house "Falling Water." It soon became world-famous.

Suddenly, at 70, his career was back on track, and he began to be regarded as America's foremost architect. The Museum of Modern Art, which had humiliated him a few years earlier, was now keen to devote an exhibition to his work. You can imagine his wry smile when he got the invitation!

At 80, Frank Lloyd Wright entered the most productive phase of his career, designing an unending stream of buildings. But he was still waiting for the big project that would cap his life. He was finally commissioned to design the Guggenheim Museum on 5th Avenue in New York. It was his most difficult project and took thirteen years to plan and build.

Finally, the ground was broken and the museum began to be built. Wright was nearly 90 at the time, but still supervised the building in all its details. He was full of vitality, right to the end.

Wright said, "To me, *young* has no meaning, it's something you can do nothing about. But *youth* is a quality, and if you have it, you never lose it."

Reflection

As Frank Lloyd Wright indicated, youthfulness has no age limit.

One of the hallmarks of inner youthfulness is vitality.

Physical vitality awakens feelings of energy and competence. Mental and spiritual vitality make us feel radiantly alive and leads to meaningful action. Inner youthfulness also manifests through being open-minded, having a sense of humor, and being playful.

What aspects of youthfulness would you like to develop?

> *"I believe youth can last a lifetime. Inner youthfulness is not a matter of our physical age. Rather, it is determined by the passion with which we live, the enthusiasm with which we learn, the freshness and energy with which we advance toward our chosen goals in life."*
> ~Daisaku Ikeda

The Unexpected Blessing of Resilience

*E*very life has peaks as well as troughs. The following story shows that resilience is the key to overcoming difficult times, recovering from setbacks, and growing as a human being.

Christopher Foster and his wife Joy had just celebrated their twenty-fifth wedding anniversary in the Caribbean and were flying back to Canada. One hour out from Vancouver, Joy suffered a massive stroke.

Chris later wrote in his journal, "How shall I forget standing in the aisle of the aircraft beside you, …the way your head rolled on its neck as you looked up at me and then away, the way your eyes saw me but did not see me, the way your ears heard but did not hear as I called and called softly, incessantly, urgently, trying to reach you, trying to awaken us both from a nightmare." Joy was rushed to a hospital as soon as the plane landed, but she died a few hours later without regaining consciousness.

As you can imagine, it was a dark time for Christopher Foster. The world he had known for decades had crumbled. But then, something marvelous happened: he met JoAnn, who was to become his second wife. "I was in a pile of despair when I met JoAnn," Chris said, "and she gave me a new lease of life."

However, seven years later, at 73, depression struck out of the blue, heralded by an anxiety attack: "I was in excellent health, happily married, and living a full and happy life—or so I thought—when I felt a sudden pounding in my chest. I decided to lie down and found myself prostrated on my bed with a major anxiety attack. My wife, JoAnn, held me for nearly three hours as I drifted in and out of consciousness, reliving, as far as we could tell, memories of experiences I had in the early days of the London Blitz before I was evacuated."

In his book, *The Secret Promise of Aging*, Chris recalls the Blitz: "I will never forget the terror I felt as our building began to sway to and fro in the blast and I clung to my mother for dear life. Nor will I ever forget how she kept saying, 'It's all right, it's all right,' as bombs continued to fall. Where did she find the strength?"

After his anxiety attack, Chris spiraled into depression and despair. He wrote, "Soon after that evening, my weight began to drop steadily. Within a few months, I was in such a poor and fragile state that I was not sure I would survive. I seemed to be on a downward slide that nothing could interrupt."

But Chris had a potential lifeline.

During childhood, in the scary time of the London *Blitz*, Christopher had developed a skill that not only helped him at the time but also became a lifelong habit: writing.

"I wrote my first story in an old scrapbook when I was a child in London in the early days of the Blitz, shortly before I was evacuated to live with an aunt in North Devon. I would have been about eight years old. I still remember the thrill I felt as I scribbled away in that old scrapbook. It was probably the first time I consciously let my imagination run wild as I developed a story out of 'thin air.'"

Was Chris going to find the resilience to lift himself out of that darkness that suddenly descended at age 73?

During his depression, he continued to write. Putting words on a page became a way of making sense of his life and helped him recover from setbacks. It became his way to trigger resilience.

After nine months, the depression lifted just as quickly as it had begun: "I emerged from the whole terrifying experience stronger and healthier than before I got sick. I threw away my medications. I began working out at the gym and putting on muscle. I discovered how to smile again, and how to laugh. But that wasn't all. I began to experience an entirely new sense of peace and well-being."

Christopher used his writing skills to overcome his latest setback. He was diagnosed with colon cancer in 2013, at age 81. After a colonoscopy, a biopsy revealed that he had stage II cancer and needed an operation. Like all cancer sufferers, Christopher experienced a lot of fear.

You could imagine that after this series of disasters, a person would feel anxious, unhappy, and maybe bitter. But the opposite happened in Christopher's case. In an interview with the American Cancer Society[3], he explained, "Anxiety still comes up, but I do find that the fear can help me uncover more of the fundamental joy of being, the joy of life itself, that for me was covered over for a lot of my life. I think in trying to suppress my fear, I suppressed my joy. Conversely, now that I'm facing the fear—the joy has been increasing. I'm a

---

[3] https://www.cancer.org/latest-news/colon-cancer-survivor-says-routine-screening-saved-his-life.html

pretty happy guy now."

I got to know Christopher in 2009 when he became one of my blogging students at age 77. At that time, the Internet was something of a mystery to him, and he initially struggled with all the skills he had to master as a new blogger. However, as a *youthful ager*, Chris was determined to create a successful blog to share his wisdom with the world.

He has since gathered a dedicated following at his blog, *TheHappySeeker.com*. His work as a blogger has allowed him to become a successful author and he has published multiple books. I interviewed him for this book, and it was exciting to see that Christopher is still focused on developing as a human being, as well as on honing his writing skills.

Christopher Foster emerged from each trough with more joy and with a deeper appreciation of life. As he said recently: "I'm happier and more fulfilled now than I have ever been in my whole life."

Growth happens when we leave our comfort zone behind, learn something new, and develop as a person. And, as Christopher shows, that's a key to enjoying life as a *youthful ager*.

Reflection

Christopher Foster is a great example of the power of positive plasticity, the human capacity to adapt, change, and grow at any age.

The two main aspects of positive plasticity are resilience and growth.

Mental resilience is the ability to recover from setbacks or trauma and keep going in the face of adversity. Physical resilience is the body's ability to bounce back from hardship, illness, or injury.

Resilience makes you elastic like a rubber ball. You can compress a ball, but when you let go, it quickly returns to its original shape. In the same way, resilience can help you return to your previous state of being after a physical, mental, or emotional challenge.

However, resilience doesn't help you adapt to change. It simply returns you to your previous condition. That's where growth, the second aspect of positive plasticity, comes into play. Growth is the process of developing physically, mentally, or spiritually. This unfolding allows you to change your configuration, like an acorn transforming into a seedling and then growing into an oak tree.

We grow as human beings when we leave our comfort zone behind, learn something new, and develop as a person.

How would you rate the qualities of resilience and growth in your life?

> "Do not judge me by my success, judge me by how many times I fell down and got back up again."
> ~Nelson Mandela

10 *Who is the Naked You?*

*A*re you the real *you*, or somebody else's version of you?

Throughout life, we are told how we *should* be. Our parents, caregivers, teachers, friends, and colleagues all exert a subtle pressure on us to conform to their idea of who we should be. And when we deviate from their norms, we can face repercussions.

One time, when I was working as a psychotherapist in Nelson, a small town of sixty thousand inhabitants, Grant Sterling, a renowned photographer, came to see me. Sitting on the couch, he fidgeted, and it took a while for him to say what was on his mind.

He cleared his throat. "I wonder if you would mind having your photo taken for a calendar to raise money for the local women's shelter?"

My eyebrows shot up. "Grant, are you asking me to be in a nudie calendar?"

"Well, yes," he stuttered. "It's going to be photos of leading women in Nelson, and the shots would be without clothes…but very, very tasteful," he added hurriedly.

"Oh, what fun!" I said. "I'm in my fifties. What a fantastic time to be in a nudie calendar!"

He sighed with relief. "I've asked a few women already, and I had a hard time talking them into it. Nobody was as enthusiastic as you about the idea!"

The photo he shot showed me reclining full-length on a couch holding a pen, and a notebook covering my essential parts.

Shortly after the calendar was published, I had a session with my psychotherapy supervisor. His face was grim. "How could you?" he said, shaking his head. "How could you let yourself to be photographed naked for all your clients to see?"

"Well," I said, shrugging, "maybe they'll get a glimpse of who I really am."

My inspiration to reveal the *real me* comes from Toni Morrison, America's most celebrated novelist. She was born in 1931.

Her first novel, *The Bluest Eye*, was published in 1970. It is about a black girl made to feel so ugly by the culture around her that she wishes for blue eyes.

As Toni Morrison explained in an interview with the *Guardian*[4], the idea for a story came out of an early encounter. When she was 12, a classmate confided to her the same dream of blue eyes. "I wanted to know how she got to that place," Morrison said.

---

[4] https://www.theguardian.com/books/2012/apr/13/toni-morrison-home-son-love

Even though her first book fell flat, Toni Morrison later became a leading novelist and editor, as well as a professor at Princeton University. She won the Pulitzer Prize and the American Book Award for her novel *Beloved*.

Later, Morrison won the Nobel Prize in Literature at age 62. She was the first African American woman to win it.

Now in her 80s, age hasn't blunted her creativity. Toni Morrison's latest novel, *God Help the Child*, was published in 2015.

But her life wasn't without challenges. Growing up in poverty, she struggled to find an identity that was not imposed from without but was true to how she felt within.

"I'm not somebody else's version of who I am," Toni Morrison said.

In her novel *Song of Solomon*, the protagonist says, "You wanna fly, you got to give up the shit that weighs you down."

The disapproval of others can wear us down. It's hard to hear those nearest to us saying, "I'm really disappointed in you." Or, "You shouldn't be doing this!" Letting go of someone else's version of who we are is challenging, but in the process, we develop authenticity.

Authenticity means being in the *now*. It means experiencing the moment right now directly, without slipping into memories of the past or dreams of the future. Toni Morrison said, "I want to feel what I feel. Even if it's not happiness."

For Morrison, a "happy place" is "…the acquisition of knowledge. If you know something at the end that you didn't know before, it's almost wisdom. And if I can hit that chord, then everything else was worth it."

How old are you, *inside?* How old is the *Naked You?*

The most important thing as we mature is to be open. Toni Morrison said, "Some people just close when they get old," she says. "But if you're open, you can rely on the lived wisdom of the elderly. It's not the book learning, it's the lived wisdom."

"I ask friends of mine, 'How old are you, *inside*?' And they always know. I know that I am 23. There's a moment when you just arrive."

The beauty of *youthful aging* is that we can experience the freedom of openness. We can let go of both the fear of failure and the pressure to succeed. We can try new things and fail or triumph, all the while finding out who we are in our naked glory, stripped of expectations.

How old you feel is one of the defining factors of how your mature years will unfold. Sometimes, the expectations of society make us think of ourselves as less valuable than younger people and unable to make the second half of our life as good as or better than the first half. But, like Morrison, we need to rise above such preconceptions. She attacks life as if she were still 23, despite being well past 85.

The "naked you" is the one you've always been. Holding on to that self-knowledge and living it to the fullest is one of the standout secrets of youthful aging.

Reflection

The "naked you" appears when your thoughts, feelings, and actions are all in harmony.

The key to such authenticity is to be fully present in the now. When we are mindful of the present moment, instead being lost in thoughts of the past or worries of the future, we learn to be at ease with ourselves just as we are.

Mindfulness helps us translate our values into action and live authentically. To practice being unconditionally present with whatever is happening, sit quietly for five minutes. Notice your breath flowing in and out, experience the feeling of your body, and become aware of ambient sounds. When your thoughts take you away, gently refocus on the experience of the present moment.

If you practice mindfulness regularly, you will be more peaceful. You will also become less self-conscious and more spontaneous.

"The privilege of a lifetime is to become who you truly are."
~Carl Jung

Light the *Fire Within*

11

*T*his story is about a farmer from Montana who decided to challenge himself and light the fire within. What happened will astound you.

In our Western society, people expect you to take it easy once you get to retirement age. When I started my experiment of embarking on five months of CrossFit training to see how a 70-year-old body would respond to an extreme exercise regimen, people around me were worried. "Shouldn't you take it easy?" they said. Or, "Are you sure that's good for you?" However, I found that this experiment lit a fire within and changed my life.

Bob Hayes, a farmer in Montana, started running in his 60s because his children talked him into it. "They kept bugging me to run," Bob said, "and they finally talked me into doing a race." He didn't realize that this would change his life completely.

At the time, the old town schoolhouse in Evero, where Bob lives, needed a renovation, and a group of community members decided to put on a race to raise money.

Bob's son Tom said, "Come on, Dad, join me for the race." Bob agreed, but he struggled to complete the distance. Afterward, Bob felt every one of his sixty years. He thought, "I wasn't feeling as fit as I would have liked to. Perhaps age is catching up with me?"

Even though the race was hard, Bob enjoyed the camaraderie of the runners and decided to join the local running club. Some months later, Bob took part in a half-marathon. That's when he realized that running longer distances was what he enjoyed most.

Fast forward ten years. At 70, Bob Hayes completed the fearsome LeGrizz 50-mile ultra-marathon. And by the time he was 83, he had completed the LeGrizz twelve times.

At age 83, Bob said, "I'm in the best shape of my life!" Now in his 90s, he still runs between 40 and 50 miles a week. "I figure I have to keep running whether I like it or not because I know that if I stop running that'll be the end of me."

During the day, Bob works his 180 acres of fields, timberland, and pasture, chopping firewood, raising animals, and laying out hay, doing things the hard way to remain active and alive. In 2016, filmmakers Erik Petersen and Jeremy Lurgio created a film about Bob Hayes, *The Hard Way: An Ultra Runner Pushes 90.*

Bob Hayes is a shining example of how taking up a personal challenge can help you gain vitality and strength, no matter how old or young you are. Let's take a look at what choosing a personal challenge could mean in everyday life. If you live or work in a high-rise building, you could walk up at least one story, instead of using the lift. When going for a walk, you could push yourself to walk fast, instead of strolling. Taking up a personal challenge doesn't mean becoming a star athlete; it means pushing yourself to do things that are difficult for you.

Bob Hayes's story shows you can build up your fitness and strength at any age. If you start exercising regularly, you can achieve an excellent level of fitness, even though you might not become a world-class athlete. Being fit makes you feel great about yourself and boosts your health. It also makes you feel younger.

Bob Hayes said, "When I'm out there in a race I never think how old I am, I think I'm the same age as the people running around me, so if they're 25, I think I'm 25 and, if they're 55, I think I'm 55, so it keeps you young."

Bob clearly shows that lighting the fire within by building a habit of challenging ourselves is a successful pathway to *youthful aging*.

Reflection

Bob Hayes is someone who always welcomed a challenge.

To face a challenge is difficult, because we all suffer from inertia, the tendency is to do nothing or to remain unchanged. Each one of us has a strong desire to stay within our comfort zones because we feel safe and secure in what we know. What happens when we step out of our areas of comfort?

In 1908, psychologists Robert M. Yerkes and John D. Dodson conducted a famous experiment in which they demonstrated that a certain amount of stress increases our productivity. Daniel H. Pink, author of *Drive: The Surprising Truth About What Motivates Us* called this stress "productive discomfort."

Every time you step out of your comfort zone, you experience this discomfort—but you also grow. In time, you find that this "productive discomfort" allows your skills to develop and your comfort zone to expand.

Next time you are challenged to try something new, try taking a small step out of your comfort zone.

> *"Whenever you feel uncomfortable, instead of retreating back into your old comfort zone, pat yourself on the back and say, "I must be growing," and continue moving forward."*
> ~T. Harv Eker

12 *A Time For Adventure?*

When they were close to retirement age, Beryl and Miles Smeeton decided to settle down in a seaside port in England. Their idea was to buy a peaceful cottage and enjoy a quiet retirement.

Miles and Beryl found a cottage they liked. But then something happened that changed the trajectory of their lives.

One day, going for a walk on the wharf, they happened to see a 46-foot ocean-going ketch. The couple strolled past, looking at it. They weren't sailors but agreed that the boat looked beautiful.

Suddenly, Beryl saw a "for sale" sign hanging on the mast. Her eyes lit up, and she turned to Miles, "Oh, wouldn't that be fun?!" Beryl and Miles grinned at each other. Shortly afterward, they decided to buy the *Tzu Hang* despite never having sailed before. But there was a problem. The owner, Denis Swinburne, had changed his mind about selling her.

However, Swinburne hadn't reckoned with Smeeton—who like him was a military man—being used to getting his way. Here is a peek into their correspondence.

Dear Swinburne,
I should very much like to buy your boat.
How much do you want for her?
Yours sincerely,
Miles Smeeton, Brigadier.

Dear Brigadier,
My boat is not for sale.
Yours sincerely,
Denis Swinburne, Colonel

Dear Swinburne,
You have not answered my question.
Yours sincerely
Miles Smeeton, Brigadier.

In the end, Swinburne accepted defeat, and the deal was struck.

Beryl and Miles were excited about learning a whole new set of skills and starting a new life, instead of "settling down" for their retirement years. They studied hard, learning how to handle the boat and how to navigate.

One of their first trips "to learn to sail" was from London to Vancouver!

This wasn't their first adventure together. The couple had met in India when they were in their early 30s. A few weeks before Miles was due to depart to England, they went on a morning walk near Poona. Beryl asked Miles how he was getting home.

"Oh, I don't know. I'm broke, so I'll most likely get a 2nd class berth on a boat."

Beryl looked at him in disbelief. "How awful," she said. "How perfectly awful!"

"So how would you go?" Miles asked, realizing that she wasn't shocked by the 2nd class passage.

"Why, overland of course!"

A few weeks later, they set off on their 10,000-kilometer journey from India to England, traveling on the cheap, eating local food and often sleeping under the stars. They used local buses, donkeys, and bicycles, hitched rides on lorries, or tagged onto camel caravans to cross the desert.

This pair was well matched. Both had a love of exploring and egged each other on to "just do it."

You might imagine that they lost their thirst for adventure when they came into their retirement years, but, as the following story shows, the pair became even more gung-ho as they matured.

Five years after buying the *Tzu Hang*, they were sailing around the world with a young friend of theirs, John Guzwell, when disaster struck.

They wanted to sail around Cape Horn from west to east—a feat that only a few boats the size of the *Tzu Hang* had ever managed to achieve without foundering.

For Beryl Smeeton, the nightmare started when she took the helm of the yacht. They were near the Magellan Straits, the most dangerous stretch of water in the world.

A storm had come up. Suddenly, there was an ominous change in the sea. Beryl recalled, "I looked over my shoulder and thought, at first, that my sight had gone. Behind me, the whole horizon was blotted out by a huge, gray wall. I was looking at a wall of vertical water."

Beryl felt the stern rise and was flung forward as the boat started to careen down the wave. Just before she lost consciousness, she realized that the boat was going to roll end over end. Next thing Beryl knew, she was in the water, struggling to fight her way to the surface. Her lifeline had broken, and she couldn't see the yacht.

"The boat is gone," she thought, struggling to keep afloat. She was badly injured, with broken ribs, a fractured shoulder blade, and a gash on her face. Then a wave lifted her, and she caught a glimpse of the yacht.

You could hardly imagine a more desolate scene.

The waves had sliced everything off the deck of the *Tzu Hang*. Both masts, the dinghy, the wheelhouse—everything was gone. Less than a foot was showing, and waves were washing over the boat. Miles and John had miraculously survived the roll from end to end. She saw them standing on the deck in their pajamas, shoulders sagging.

Then they saw Beryl in the water.

John later said that he was so sure the *Tzu Hang* would sink at any moment that he made no effort to get Beryl on board: "I really couldn't see any point. I knew we'd be joining her soon, and I remember thinking that I might as well jump in beside her."

Meanwhile, Beryl was trying to swim toward the boat, even though she was in agonizing pain with her broken shoulder and ribs. She was in her late 60s at the time, and, even for a 20-year-old, this would have been a seemingly impossible task.

Over the roar of the storm, Miles heard her cry out to him. At first, he thought she was calling for help, but then he heard her shout, "Start bailing!" Miles looked at John in confusion. "What does she mean?" he said. Miles was dazed and confused.

When Beryl was close to the yacht, they finally managed to haul her to safety. Miles was about to give her a last hug before they died together when he realized Beryl was furious.

"What are you two doing, standing around like dolts?" she shouted.

"But Beryl," Miles said quietly, shaking his head. "There is nothing to do now. We are at the end."

"Bollocks! We need to start bailing. Now!"

Miles shook his head. "But the water in the cabin is up to my chest."

"All the more reason to start bailing! You, John, start covering the holes in the deck with pieces of sail. Miles, you come with me to start bailing!"

Beryl managed to find a bucket down below and tied a rope to it. She also found her cat Pwe desperately swimming in circles and lifted her up onto a shelf.

With her broken shoulder, she could only lift one of her arms waist high, but she started working with Miles to empty the cabin of water. They bailed for twelve hours straight.

For a long time, it was touch-and-go whether the *Tzu Hang* would sink or swim. Then the boat gradually began to rise.

How did it end?

After the ordeal in the Magellan Straits, the yacht was able to limp to the coast of Chile where Beryl, Miles and John, as well as the cat Pwe, recovered, and their ship was rebuilt.

However, this extraordinary couple didn't know the meaning of the words "give up." They certainly didn't conform to what people think a couple in their late 60s should be doing. No chair and slippers for them! Instead, they planned a new challenge.

A year later, they attempted the same voyage around Cape Horn again. And, more or less in the same position, their boat rolled and was again dismasted by a rogue wave.

They managed to survive.

And yes, you guessed it. They attempted this voyage a third time a few years later. By this time, they were pushing 70. On their third try, they successfully rounded Cape Horn.

They survived and thrived against all odds, enjoying a life of adventure, decades after they had contemplated "settling down for retirement."

As you can see, Beryl and Miles were fans of unbridled exploration with a mindset of "just do it." Miles explained, "So often, at lectures and book-signings, people would say, 'You're so lucky, I'd love to do this or that.' And I can't help saying, 'Well, why the hell don't you?'"

Reflection

Beryl and Miles were extreme adventurers; they certainly lived their dreams.

Even though you might not want to risk your life in dangerous escapades, following your dreams is important. Maybe you have dreams but have never got around to making them come true.

It can be deeply satisfying to do something you've put off, year after year. For example, I went back to university in my late 50s and completed an MA in Religious Studies on my 60th birthday. The first six months of study were hard, and I struggled to come to grips with academic work, but in the end, it was a gratifying experience.

What are some dreams you've put off?

Make a list of things you would like to do but have put off in the past.

> *"Twenty years from now, you will be more disappointed by the things you didn't do than by the ones you did do. So throw off the bowlines. Sail away from the safe harbor. Catch the trade winds in your sail. Explore. Dream. Discover."*
> ~Mark Twain

13 *Is Love Ageless?*

*H*ave you ever wondered about falling in love again? Maybe you're in a satisfying relationship, but if you're on your own, the idea of staying single can be daunting. We all fear being lonely, especially as our years accumulate. But it doesn't have to be this way.

The good news is that you can fall in love at any age and start a new, happy relationship, just like Dame Judi Dench did.

When Dame Judi was in her thirties, she was introduced to fellow actor Michael Williams. "Mutual friends of ours introduced us in a pub in Covent Garden," she says. "He had this marvelous sense of humor, which, for me, is paramount. We knew each other as friends for a long, long time…If we hadn't married, he'd still have been my best friend, which I think is kind of the secret to being happy." They married and had a daughter who she calls Finty. Michael was a true romantic and sent her a rose each Friday.

When she lost Michael to lung cancer after thirty years of marriage, her life turned dark. But she forced herself to go on. "With the help of my daughter and my grandson, who was then very little, and my friends, I got through it," she later said.

Dench was 67 at the time and was dreading the lonely years ahead. However, she never lost hope that she would fall in love, and be loved, once again.

> *"To all, I would say how mistaken they are when they think that they stop falling in love when they grow old, without knowing that they grow old when they stop falling in love."*
> ~Gabriel García Márquez

A couple of years after Michael's passing, she met conservationist David Mills, an ex-farmer who had built a wildlife center dedicated to British animals near Dame Judi's home. One day, she called in at the center.

David Mills later said, "She came here as a punter with her family in 2010. I happened to be in the office that day, saw her come in and I thought, 'Judi Dench!'"

"We got chatting, and a couple of months later I asked her to open a new red squirrel enclosure here…After that, as they say, the rest is history…"

David revealed how he experiences the relationship with Dame Judi:

"It developed as a slow, organic friendship that grew. I invited her to come and have supper one night, and then she asked me to one of her things. It's lasted because we have the same sense of humor—it's hopeless without that—and then she's passionate about wildlife, as I am about theatre and films, so we go into one another's worlds.

"She's a great giggler. We laugh and joke so much, and enjoy one another's worlds so much, it's great, especially when you get to our age. We do normal things—watch telly like everyone else. We love *Strictly* and *Blue Planet*. We go to the local cinema—most recently we saw *Dunkirk* there, because Kenny Branagh's in it. Thoroughly enjoyed that. We do quite a lot of entertaining with friends. Her red-carpet world is totally different to mine. It was daunting to begin with for a little old simple country boy who's used to milking cows. But I've met a lot of very interesting people....We share each other's worlds, which is lovely."

As you can see, the attraction between the couple is mutual and they enjoy giggling together. "I love having a good laugh," Dame Judi said. "A sense of humor is the most attractive thing of all. It's essential."

But what about passion?

It's clear that her passionate feelings reawakened in the relationship with David. Judi said, "One hot night during the summer we swam and had a glass of champagne in the garden, and I said, 'This is so fantastic.' I wasn't even prepared to be ready for it. It was very gradual and grown up...it's just wonderful," she said.

At 82, Judi Dench hinted that she still enjoys an active sex life. In an interview, the Oscar winner said, "Well, of course, you still feel desire. Does that ever go?"

Talking about Queen Victoria, whom she played in the movie *Victoria & Abdul*, Dame Judi said, "She had a huge passion and need inside her. She had a happy life with Albert and then those years with John Brown, and then I'm sure she'd certainly given up by then and was just caught up in the drudgery of everything. And suddenly, that wonderful kind of flowering, where she thought, 'This is really something worth living for.'"

Meeting her companion David Mills was a "wonderful kind of flowering" for Dame Judi. Instead of spending her mature years alone, she found new love and companionship to light up her life. She said, "It's wonderful to be in love. That state when you're glad to see somebody and they make you laugh, and you just like being with them."

This experience taught me that positive thoughts encourage us to change our lives in ways that can make new things happen.

The beautiful thing about love is that it's ageless. You are never too old to fall in love and never too old to start a new life. As Dame Judi says, "To the older reader, I would say, 'Don't give up!'"

Reflection

What can we learn from Dame Judi Dench?

I think one of the most important things is to be open to love. I was single for many years after the divorce from my first husband. Finally, at 52, I vowed to open myself to a new relationship. Six months later, I met David, the lovely partner I am still with today.

This experience taught me that positive thoughts encourage us to change our lives in ways that can make new things happen.

Whether you are on your own or with a partner, it's important to grow your capacity for love.

Start by making a list of the people closest to you and focus on what you love, admire, or appreciate about them. Whenever you feel aggrieved or irritated by someone close to you, call to mind something you appreciate about them. This will expand your ability to love.

> *"The ultimate lesson all of us have to learn is unconditional love, which includes not only others but ourselves as well."*
> ~Elisabeth Kubler-Ross

14 The Benefits of Being Audacious

Imagine going head to head with the world's foremost authorities, to save mankind...in your 80s. Crazy, right?

The renowned biologist Edward O. Wilson, Professor Emeritus at Harvard University and recipient of two Pulitzer Prizes, created a storm of controversy when he published his most audacious work at age 88. In the book *Half Earth: Our Planet's Fight for Life*, Wilson suggests humans set aside fifty percent of the planet as a permanent reserve to preserve the biodiversity of species and the future of the human race.

Publishing *Half Earth* was a bold move. You can be sure he had to step out of his comfort zone to do it.

Stepping out of your comfortable routine is challenging. However, audacious *youthful agers* have more fun, enjoy incredible experiences, and create amazing memories when they push against the boundaries of their comfort zone.

E.O. Wilson didn't stop to ask permission from anyone before publishing *Half Earth*. As the blogger Marelisa Fabrega points out, we are indoctrinated as children to ask for permission for the things we want to do. Even in adulthood, this sense of needing permission from others still lingers on. However, as *youthful agers*, the only permission we need is from ourselves!

When *Half Earth* was published, it immediately triggered a vicious debate but Edward Wilson was ready for it. In an interview with the Smithsonian[5], he said, "Battles are where the fun is and where the most rapid advances are made."

The controversy reminded Wilson of a time he was suddenly flung from his dreamy, playful childhood into the hostile environment of a boarding school. This reversal started when Edward was 7 years old. That's when he became a bold battler.

Because his parents were embroiled in divorce proceedings, they sent their boy to the Gulf Coast Military Academy, a private boarding school. When he arrived there with his mother, the grounds looked inviting. However, the reality was very different. E.O. Wilson later described his first impression in his autobiography, *Naturalist*:

"We entered the Junior Dormitory to meet the housemother and some of the other grammar-school cadets. I looked at my military-style cot, the kind you can bounce a coin on when properly made, I listened to an outline of the daily regime. I examined my uniform, patterned after that at West Point. I shook hands with my roommate, who was inordinately stiff and polite for a seven-year-old. Any dreams of languor and boyhood dreams vanished."

---

[5] https://www.smithsonianmag.com/science-nature/can-world-really-set-aside-half-planet-wildlife-180952379/

He later said the Gulf Coast Military Academy was "a carefully planned nightmare engineered for the betterment of the untutored and undisciplined."

After his time at the Academy, his father dragged young Edward around from city to city, moving almost every year. In each new school, Edward had to face down bullies—who liked to pick on him because he had lost some of his eyesight in a fishing accident.

Despite all of these challenges, he developed an abiding love of nature. At university, E.O. Wilson studied biology, specializing in entomology, the study of insects. He then became a member of Harvard's biology faculty. But Wilson wasn't satisfied with focusing on a narrow subject; he became interested in sociobiology, the study of the genetic basis of the social behavior of all animals (including humans).

According to the *Guardian*, Jared Diamond (who also won a Pulitzer Prize) described Wilson as "one of the 20th century's greatest thinkers." Biologist Richard Dawkins praised Wilson's breadth of vision: "He is hugely learned, not just in his field of social insects, but in anthropology and other subjects as well. He is an outstanding synthesizer, his knowledge is immense, and he manages to bring it all together in a coherent way."

Many critics panned E.O. Wilson's book *Half Earth*, calling it an "improbable prescription for the environment." In an interview with the *New York Times*, Wilson was asked, "Do you worry that you are risking the reputation of a lifetime with such a controversial proposal?" He replied, "Controversy doesn't bother me. I don't think I'm risking my reputation with *Half Earth*. All I'm doing is reporting good science and the experiences of researchers who've described a biodiversity crisis."

E.O. Wilson's story can inspire us to become more audacious and less cautious. Being bold and irrepressible, we bring more excitement and joy into our lives!

When faced with restrictions, ask, "Are all of these rules really necessary?" And, "What is my gut telling me to do?" For E.O. Wilson, writing *Half Earth* "his own way" meant grappling with a range of revolutionary ideas and then piecing the new concepts together to form a coherent blueprint. You can imagine how taxing such a project was for his brain.

In an article in the *New York Times*,[6] Professor Lisa Feldman has this to say about developing the brain of what she calls a "superager": "Pleasant puzzles like Sudoku are not enough to provide the benefits of superaging. Neither are the popular diversions of various 'brain game' websites. You must expend enough effort that you feel some 'yuck.' Do it till it hurts, and then a bit more."

The most important point here is that we are capable of revitalizing the brain, even if it means going for the mental "ouch factor." But nothing is achieved without daring to shine.

---

[6] https://www.nytimes.com/2016/12/31/opinion/sunday/how-to-become-a-superager.html

Reflection

E.O. Wilson's story can inspire us to become more audacious and less cautious. When we are bold and irrepressible, we experience excitement and joy.

In her article "How to Be More Daring, Bold and Audacious," Marelisa Fabrega suggests a simple strategy for becoming audacious: break the rules.

When faced with restrictions, ask, "Are all of these rules really necessary?" And, "What is my gut telling me to do?"

As a *youthful ager,* make up your own rules and do things your own way.

When I first started CrossFit training at age 70, my friends were sceptical. They said, "Should you really be doing this at your age?" But I was determined to take on a new challenge.

When I first arrived at the CrossFit gym for my first lesson, trainers and students looked at me askance. However, a short time later, everyone forgot about my age, and they now see me for what I am: a motivated and enthusiastic student.

Are there are areas in your life where you have held back because of pressure from others?

How could you be more audacious?

"Whatever you can do,
or dream you can,
begin it. Boldness has genius,
power and magic in it."
~Johann Wolfgang von Goethe

15 This Moment, the Youth of Your Future

A short while ago, a woman in her late forties approached me with a troubled look. "I'm noticing the first signs of menopause," she said. "Is this the beginning of the end?"

"No," I said. "It's the start of freedom!"

Everyone feels afraid of aging at times. As we go through life, it's easy to think that the good years are behind us. Even people in their thirties can start to feel they are on a downhill slide when they see younger people zap past them at work or on the playing field.

But imagine for a moment what your life could be like in 10, 30, or 40 years! What will you have accomplished, what dreams will you have made real? What will you be proud of? How will it feel when younger people treat you as a friend and guide?

Imagine, in your future years, when you're asked about your life, being able, like Charles Eugster, to say: "It's absolutely marvelous, it's stupendous, it's terrific, amazing, exciting!"

The stories of *youthful agers* I've collected in this book are like beacons to guide us through our future. When we feel like flagging, we can remember Grandma Moses sitting propped up on pillows, painting doggedly, day after day. When a task feels overwhelming, we can think of Cliff Young in his boots and torn trousers at the start of his epic race.

One vital lesson shines through all the stories of these *youthful agers*: positive thoughts about the capacity of your body and mind translate directly into growth and healing, whereas negative expectations of the future diminish our competence in every way.

In the *New York Times* article, renowned psychologist Professor Lisa Feldman was asked how people can become what she calls *superagers*:

"Our best answer at the moment is: work hard at something. Many labs have observed that critical brain regions increase in activity when people perform difficult tasks, whether the effort is physical or mental. You can, therefore, help keep these regions thick and healthy through vigorous exercise and bouts of strenuous mental effort."

Whenever we embrace a mental or physical challenge, we are on the pathway to *youthful aging*. Whenever we feel the *ouch factor*, we know that mind and body are rejuvenating.

No matter how old or young you are, there is no time like the present to start your journey of becoming a *youthful ager*. The first step is to change your perception of the mature chapter of life.

Becoming a *youthful ager* means anticipating and enjoying a time of life when you can learn, wonder, explore, experiment, play, and create in order to develop in every possible way. The process of *youthful aging* is a personal revolution that awakens the potential within you and sets you free. This revolution doesn't happen overnight, though; it takes a series of steps to rejuvenate body, mind, and spirit. The *Youthful Aging* series will guide you each step of the way.

Join the *youthful aging* movement. Let's stand tall against people who think that aging makes a person less able and less valuable. Let's make the mature chapter of our lives the best time ever!

> *In terms of days and moments lived, you'll never again be as young as you are right now, so spend this day, the youth of your future, in a way that deflects regret. Invest in yourself. Have some fun. Do something important. Love somebody extra. In one sense, you're just a kid, but a kid with enough years on you to know that every day is priceless."*
> ~ Victoria Moran

The next step is to rejuvenate your body. In the next book in the *Youthful Aging* series, **Fountain of Youth: The 30 Minute Workout Week,** you'll be guided, step by step, to rejuvenate your body and get your bounce back. I'll share with you some exciting research results.

See you there.

FOR THE READER

Thank you so much for downloading my book!

I really appreciate your support and feedback, and I love hearing what you have to say. Please leave me a helpful review on Amazon. As a "thank-you", I'd like to give you a workbook that you can download for free. This workbook will help you create a vision of what you want your life to be like going forward.

You can get the workbook here: *goodlifezen.com/ya-workbook/*

ACKNOWLEDGEMENTS

Many people supported me in writing this book. I'd like to acknowledge the invaluable help of my wonderful Editor, Laura Tong, whose supportive guidance made the process of creation smooth and enjoyable.

I'd also like to thank my partner, David Bagshaw, as well as my son, Sebastian Grodd, for believing in me and urging me on.

I'm also deeply indebted to my *Youthful Aging Posse,* the group of engaged readers whose feedback enhanced the shape of this book.

ABOUT THE AUTHOR

Mary Jaksch is an inspiring example of someone who takes no notice of words, like 'too old' or 'too difficult.' An author, blogger, and Zen Master, Mary is a 5th degree Blackbelt in karate. Her book *Learn to Love* was published in seven countries. In line with her inspiring message of *youthful aging,* Mary started CrossFit at age 70 and competes internationally. Nevertheless, she has an abiding weakness for chocolate.

Her book *Youthful Aging Secrets* has started a revolution which is changing the way people perceive the mature part of life. You can read more by Mary on her blogs, Goodlifezen.com and Writetodone.com where she reaches over three million readers.